How to Negotiate with Microsoft

Proven Strategies to help you Maximise Value and Minimise Costs

Mark Bartrick

Copyright © 2023 Mark Bartrick

ISBN: 978-1-916820-13-5

All rights reserved, including the right to reproduce this book, or portions thereof in any form. No part of this text may be reproduced, transmitted, downloaded, decompiled, reverse engineered, or stored, in any form or introduced into any information storage and retrieval system, in any form or by any means, whether electronic or mechanical without the express written permission of the author.

About the Author

Mark Bartrick is a negotiation coach and lives in Leicestershire in the UK.

He has been helping businesses negotiate contracts for over 30 years.

Mark has worked as a Negotiation Consultant for Gartner Inc, and was also a Sourcing and Vendor Management Analyst at Forrester Research Inc. As well as publishing research about negotiation and sourcing best practices, Mark also helped many Gartner and Forrester clients save money by teaching them how to negotiate better deals with their software and technology suppliers.

Mark now has his own negotiation consulting business which specialises in helping CIOs and IT Procurement leaders negotiate better deals with enterprise software vendors such as Microsoft, Oracle, SAP and Salesforce.

You can contact Mark via his business website www.scr21.co.uk or message him via his Profile page on LinkedIn.

Who is this Book for?

This book is aimed at every business or organisation that uses Microsoft software and associated services.

It will especially appeal to any CIOs, IT Directors or Heads of Procurement who are keen to optimise their budgets and drive maximum value from their spend with Microsoft.

There's no doubt that Microsoft's software and services are both popular and useful. Many businesses and organisations across the world use Microsoft products and services, and Microsoft is often deeply embedded in many daily work tasks.

That leaves many IT and Procurement leaders thinking they are powerless when it comes to negotiating a better deal with Microsoft.

But that's not the case.

Even when Microsoft is the only game in town there are still many negotiation levers you can use to get them to move on contractual terms, pricing, discounts and concessions.

This book will help you prepare, plan and then optimise your next Microsoft negotiation.

Contents:

Chapter 1: Introduction to Microsoft   1

- Company History   1
- Financials   2
- Sales Channels   5
- Sales Culture   6

Chapter 2: Microsoft's Products/Services   8

- Product and Service Overview   8
- Software   8
- Microsoft Cloud   12
- Services   12

Chapter 3: Microsoft's Pricing   16

- List Prices   16
- Pricing Variances   17

Chapter 4: Microsoft's Paperwork   20

- Contracts & Agreements   20
- Software Support Contracts   23
- Software Assurance   24
- Premier Support   26
- Unified Support   28
- Azure Cloud Contracts   30
- Services Contracts   33

Chapter 5: Negotiation preparation   37

- Do your Homework   37
- Key Elements to Consider   38
- Microsoft's Sales Process   42
- Managing your Microsoft Sales Rep   45

Chapter 6: Negotiating Paperwork   49

- Always Take Legal Advice   49
- Microsoft Software Contracts   50
- Microsoft Cloud Contracts   54
- Microsoft Services Contracts   57

Chapter 7: Negotiating Software Pricing   62

- Discount Options   62
- Negotiating Trade-in Credits   65
- Negotiating True-ups/downs   67

Chapter 8: Negotiating Support Costs   70

- Microsoft Support   70
- Software Assurance   70
- Support Costs for SaaS   72
- Unified Support   73

Chapter 9: Negotiating Cloud Costs   **77**

- Factors that Affect Azure Cloud Pricing   77
- Azure Cloud Negotiation   79
- Azure Discounting   82
- Cloud Contract Nuances   84
- Microsoft's Cloud Competitors   85

Chapter 10: Negotiating Services Costs   **87**

- Steps to Take   87
- Services Discounts   89

Chapter 11: Bringing It All Together   **92**

- Negotiate the Total Price   92
- Negotiating Beyond Price   93

Chapter 12: Post Sale   **96**

- Post-Negotiation Relationships are Important   96
- Strategies for Maintaining Good Relationships with Microsoft   96
- Dealing with Potential Conflicts   97

Chapter 13: Negotiating Audits   **99**

- Audits are Inevitable   99
- The Importance of SAM   100
- Negotiating an Audit   100

Chapter 14: Conclusion   **104**

Chapter 1:

Introduction to Microsoft

Company History:

Microsoft Corporation is an American multinational technology corporation headquartered in Redmond, Washington. It is one of the largest software companies in the world, with over 200,000 employees.

Microsoft's best-known software products are the Windows line of operating systems, the Microsoft Office suite, and the Internet Explorer, Bing and Edge web browsers. Its flagship hardware products are the Xbox video game consoles and the Microsoft Surface lineup of touchscreen personal computers.

Microsoft was founded by Bill Gates and Paul Allen on April 4, 1975. It then rose to dominate the personal computer operating system market with MS-DOS in the mid-1980s, followed by Windows. The company's 1986 initial public offering (IPO) and subsequent rise in its share price created three billionaires and an estimated 12,000 millionaires among Microsoft employees.

Since the 1990s, it has increasingly diversified from the operating system market and has made a number of corporate acquisitions, their largest being the acquisition of LinkedIn for $26.2 billion in December 2016.

In addition, Microsoft also offers a variety of cloud services marketed under the name Azure. These cloud services allow organizations to run their applications and store their data in a secure and scalable environment, while minimizing the need for expensive on-premises hardware and IT resources.

More recently, starting in 2019, Microsoft has been developing a long-term partnership with OpenAI to accelerate Artificial Intelligence (AI) breakthroughs. These will include new AI-powered experiences across Microsoft's consumer and enterprise software products, and developments of new supercomputers to help power the AI world.

Microsoft has clearly established itself as a leader in the enterprise software market.

Financials:

In the financial year ending June 30th, 2023, Microsoft reported revenues of $211.9 billion. This was a 7% increase on the prior year. Net income was $72.4 billion.

Broken down by product groups, Microsoft's revenues for the year ending June 2023 were generated as follows:

Productivity & Business Processes: $69,274 million

Intelligent Cloud: $87,907 million

More Personal Computing: $54,734 million

The Productivity and Business Processes segment consists of products and services for productivity, communication, and information services. This segment primarily comprises:

- Office Commercial which includes Microsoft 365 and Office 365 subscriptions, and Office licensed on-premises.

- Office Consumer which includes Microsoft 365 Consumer subscriptions, Office licensed on-premises, and other Office services.

- LinkedIn.

- Dynamics business solutions which include Dynamics 365, Power Apps, on-premises ERP and CRM applications.

The Intelligent Cloud segment consists of various public, private, and hybrid server products and cloud services. This segment primarily comprises:

•	Server products and cloud services including Azure and other cloud services such as SQL Server, Windows Server, Visual Studio, System Center, and related Client Access Licenses ("CALs").

•	Enterprise Services includes Enterprise Support Services, Industry Solutions (formerly Microsoft Consulting Services), and Nuance professional services.

The More Personal Computing segment consists of:

•	Windows, including Windows Operating System, Windows cloud services, and other Windows commercial offerings such as patent licensing and Windows Internet of Things.

•	Devices, including Surface, HoloLens, and PC accessories.

•	Gaming, including Xbox hardware and Xbox content, services and subscriptions, Xbox Cloud Gaming, as well as advertising and royalties.

- Search and news advertising which includes Bing (and Bing Chat), Microsoft News, Microsoft Edge, and third-party affiliates.

> ***Negotiation Tip*** *-Microsoft is ultra-sensitive to any deals that conclude close to their key financial dates such as Quarter Ends, Half Year and (most importantly) their Financial Year End on June 30th. Timing your Microsoft contract renewal to occur at or near one of Microsoft's key financial dates can be a source of leverage for a canny buyer.*

Sales Channels:

While individuals and small organisations can buy Microsoft software from Microsoft's own online store as well as from a multitude of physical and online third-party retailers, PC sellers, partners and resellers, larger enterprises and organisations can expect to interact with Microsoft sales reps directly.

This book focusses on negotiating directly with Microsoft and the Microsoft sales rep, as they are the ones that can significantly amend pricing and terms during any contract negotiation.

Partners/Resellers/Retailers have limited scope to change much in any Microsoft deal, hence the need for enterprise buyers to focus most of their attention on Microsoft and its sales reps.

Sales Culture:

A significant factor contributing to Microsoft's success is its sales culture, which can be summarised as a combination of customer-centricity, innovation, and a results-driven approach.

One of the key aspects of Microsoft's sales culture is its emphasis on customer-centricity. The company places a strong emphasis on understanding customer needs and providing solutions that address those needs. This customer-centric approach fosters trust and long-term relationships with clients, which is crucial in the technology industry where customer loyalty and satisfaction are paramount.

Innovation is another cornerstone of Microsoft's sales culture. The company is known for its continuous investment in research and development, resulting in a growing portfolio of popular products and services.

Microsoft's sales culture also places a strong emphasis on accountability and results. The company sets ambitious targets for its sales teams and provides them with the necessary resources and support to achieve those goals. Sales reps at Microsoft are empowered to take ownership of their targets and are held accountable for their performance. The company fosters a competitive environment where individuals are encouraged to exceed expectations and drive revenue growth. Regular performance reviews, goal setting, and recognition programs are implemented to motivate and reward high achievers.

Chapter 2

Microsoft's Products & Services

Product and Services Overview:

Microsoft designs and sells a variety software and hardware products. It also offers services that complement them (such as training, support, consulting, and cloud hosting services).

The following is a list of Microsoft's main software products and associated services:

Software:

Microsoft offers a wide range of software products that cater to the various needs of individuals, businesses, and organizations. Some of the main software products sold by Microsoft include:

1. Windows Operating System: Microsoft's flagship product is the Windows operating system, which powers millions of computers worldwide. It includes versions such as Windows 11 and Windows Server, providing users with a user-friendly interface, security features, and compatibility with a vast array of software applications.

2. Microsoft Office Suite: The Microsoft Office Suite is a collection of productivity software solutions that includes applications like Microsoft Word (word processing), Excel (spreadsheet), PowerPoint (presentation), Outlook (email and calendar), and more. It is widely used in both personal and professional settings for document creation, data analysis, and communication.

3. SQL Server: This is a relational database management system (RDBMS) that enables businesses to store, manage, and analyse large amounts of structured data. It provides robust security, high availability, and scalability features, making it suitable for enterprise-level data management.

4. Dynamics 365: This is a suite of integrated business applications that help organizations manage their sales, customer service, finance, operations, and marketing functions. It provides tools for customer relationship management (CRM) and enterprise resource planning (ERP), allowing businesses to streamline their processes and improve customer engagement.

5. Visual Studio: Visual Studio is an integrated development environment (IDE) that provides developers with a comprehensive set of tools for building software applications for various platforms, including Windows, web, mobile, and cloud. It

supports multiple programming languages and frameworks, making it a popular choice among software developers.

6. SharePoint: This is a collaboration and content management platform that allows organizations to create websites, share and manage documents, and facilitate team collaboration. It provides features such as document libraries, workflows, and version control, enhancing productivity and information sharing within businesses.

7. Microsoft Teams: Microsoft Teams is a unified communication and collaboration platform that combines chat, video meetings, file sharing, and integration with other Microsoft tools. It enables teams to collaborate in real-time, irrespective of their location, making it a valuable tool for remote work and virtual meetings.

These are just a few examples of the main software products offered by Microsoft. The company also provides a range of other software solutions, including development tools, server applications, security products, and industry-specific applications, catering to the diverse needs of its customers.

Microsoft is also bringing to market their new AI-enhanced productivity software tools: Microsoft 365 CoPilot and Bing Chat AI for Enterprise.

Whether researching industry insights, analysing data, or looking for inspiration, Bing Chat AI for Enterprise will give people access to better search, better answers, greater efficiency and new ways to be creative utilising their own company's data.

Copilot will be integrated into the Microsoft 365 apps you use every day — Word, Excel, PowerPoint, Outlook, Teams and more — and its goal is to unleash creativity, unlock productivity and uplevel skills. Copilot will include Business Chat which works across the Microsoft 365 apps and your data — your calendar, emails, chats, documents, meetings and contacts — to enable customers to use natural language prompts like "Draft a proposal from yesterday's meeting notes".

This exciting use of AI will further boost Microsoft's revenues as well as make their software products even more embedded in customer's IT estates. Which makes finding negotiation leverage even more important for those customers who want the best products at a fair price.

Microsoft Cloud:

Azure is Microsoft's cloud computing platform, offering a wide range of services for building, deploying, and managing applications and services through Microsoft-managed data centres.

Azure provides infrastructure-as-a-service (IaaS), platform-as-a-service (PaaS), and software-as-a-service (SaaS) offerings, enabling organizations to develop, deploy, and scale their applications efficiently.

Services

Microsoft offers a range of professional services to its customers. These services are designed to help customers maximize the value and effectiveness of Microsoft technologies within their organizations.

Some of the main professional services offered by Microsoft include:

1. Consulting Services: Microsoft provides consulting services to assist customers in planning, designing, and implementing technology solutions. These services involve assessing business needs, creating a technology roadmap, and providing guidance on leveraging Microsoft products to achieve

specific goals. Microsoft consultants work closely with customers to understand their requirements and offer tailored recommendations for optimizing their IT infrastructure and processes.

2. Training and Certification: Microsoft offers comprehensive training programs to help individuals and organizations build expertise in Microsoft technologies. These programs include instructor-led training, online courses, and self-paced learning resources. Microsoft also provides certification programs that validate individuals' technical skills and knowledge, allowing them to demonstrate proficiency in Microsoft products and technologies.

3. Support Services: Microsoft offers various support services to assist customers in resolving technical issues and maximizing the performance of their Microsoft products. These services may include phone, email, and chat support, as well as access to an online knowledge base and community forums. Microsoft's support services aim to provide timely and effective assistance to customers, ensuring smooth operation and minimizing downtime.

4. Managed Services: Microsoft partners with managed service providers (MSPs) who offer ongoing management and support for Microsoft technologies. These MSPs help customers with tasks such as infrastructure management, system monitoring, security, and regular maintenance. Managed services

allow organizations to offload certain IT responsibilities to expert providers, freeing up internal resources and ensuring the efficient and reliable operation of Microsoft's solutions.

5. Migration and Deployment Services: Microsoft assists customers in migrating their existing systems to Microsoft technologies, such as transitioning from legacy software to the latest versions of Microsoft products or moving to the cloud using Azure. These services involve careful planning, data migration, application integration, and testing to ensure a smooth and successful transition.

6. Industry-specific Solutions: Microsoft offers industry-specific solutions and services tailored to the unique needs of various sectors, such as healthcare, finance, retail, manufacturing, and government. These solutions combine Microsoft software products with industry-specific expertise to address specific challenges and requirements within each sector.

7. Enterprise Support: Microsoft provides specialized support services for enterprise customers who have large-scale deployments and complex IT environments. Enterprise Support offers access to technical specialists, proactive monitoring, problem resolution, and guidance for optimizing performance, scalability, and security of Microsoft solutions within an enterprise context.

These professional services offered by Microsoft aim to support customers throughout their technology journey, from initial planning and implementation to ongoing management and optimization. By providing these services, Microsoft strives to ensure that customers derive maximum value from their investments in Microsoft products and achieve their business objectives effectively.

> ***Negotiation Tip:*** *Only ever buy what you need today. Don't over-buy to chase a small increment in discount. Microsoft has been known to front load deals and bundle as much product as possible in from day one. This maximises their revenues but means customers can end up paying for products/services they may not need for months or even years. This results in what's known as 'shelfware'; where licenses are not being used (e.g., left on the shelf) but are still being paid for. So a key item in any negotiation with Microsoft is to just buy what you need today and to then grow the license estate in the future as your needs grow.*

Chapter 3

Microsoft's Pricing

List Prices:

Microsoft does publish retail List prices for many of its products and services on its website.

Being able to access Microsoft's retail prices enables buyers to help set budgets and check discounts. It also allows their customers to independently assess the likely maximum costs for buying new or additional products or services. This can help with setting budgets and can help give at least a rough steer as to potential project costs without involving a Microsoft sales rep.

Enterprise buyers need to navigate past the standard retail price pages and find the specific business application pricing pages they are looking for. For example, if a buyer is looking for Office 365 enterprise list prices, then you'd need to search for 'Microsoft Office 365 prices' to find the list prices for each Office 365 option (E1, E3, F3, E5).

> **Negotiation Tip:** A quick glance at their Office 365 pricing soon reveals that there are several options (E1, E3, F3 and E5). Microsoft would love to see a customer sign up for the premium E5 version for their employees. But this is unrealistic as not all employees need all the premium features of E5. So a careful study should be undertaken by the customer's IT team to profile the customer's workforce and to identify who needs E5, who needs E3 or F3, and who only needs E1. That profile mix can then be presented to Microsoft so that they can then build an appropriate proposal with the right mix of user profiles and Office 365 licenses.

Pricing Variances:

While the specific details may vary, here are some common aspects of how Microsoft prices and discounts its software for businesses and enterprises:

1. List Price: Microsoft establishes a list price for each of its software products, which represents the standard or published price for the product.

2. Licensing Metrics: Depending on the product, there may also be a choice of licensing metric, such as enterprise, standard, per core, or developer that influences the pricing structure. The pricing will depend on the metric selected and the specific terms

associated with it. Different metrics have different pricing considerations.

3. Volume and Quantity: Microsoft offers volume discounts based on the quantity of licenses being purchased. Enterprise customers buying a larger number of licenses are eligible for tiered pricing or bulk purchase discounts. As standard, Microsoft offers four bands of volume discount (A, B, C and D) as follows:

Discount Level	Number of Users or Devices
A	500 – 2399
B	2400 – 5999
C	6000 – 14999
D	from 15000

Whether your organisation is looking at Microsoft for the first time, or is a long-standing user, it's key to keep up to date with Microsoft's pricing as it does change regularly.

Also, it's worth noting that Microsoft price lists vary by geography, so any buyer should check their local list prices and should not base their budgets on Microsoft's USA price lists.

Examples of discounts customers can target are outlined in Chapter 7.

Negotiation Tip: *Microsoft occasionally has special price promotions to encourage their sales force to sell certain products or services at a specific time. Asking your Microsoft rep or Microsoft Partner if there are any special deals available this month or coming up soon might uncover something worth pursuing if its relevant.*

Chapter 4:

Microsoft's Paperwork

Contracts & Agreements:

When an enterprise decides to purchase Microsoft software, there are typically two main types of contracts they may need to sign: the Microsoft Volume Licensing Agreement and the Microsoft Cloud Agreement. These contracts outline the terms and conditions of software licensing and usage rights, ensuring compliance and providing specific benefits to the enterprise.

Let's explore these contracts in more detail:

1. Microsoft Volume Licensing Agreement: This agreement is applicable for enterprises looking to acquire licenses for on-premises software products, such as Windows operating systems or Microsoft Office Suite. There are different types of volume licensing agreements, including:

a. Enterprise Agreement (EA): The EA is a comprehensive licensing agreement that provides organizations with a consistent and flexible way to acquire Microsoft software licenses for a large number of users or devices over a specified term (usually three years). It offers options for standardizing software across the organization, volume discounts, and additional benefits like Software Assurance, which provides upgrade rights and support services.

b. Enterprise Subscription Agreement (EAS): The EAS is similar to the EA but focused on subscription-based licensing. It allows enterprises to pay for licenses on a subscription basis, typically annually, for a specified term. This agreement is suited for organizations that prefer the flexibility of subscription licensing and want to maintain up-to-date software versions.

c. Select Plus Agreement: Select Plus is a transactional licensing program that enables enterprises to acquire licenses on a pay-as-you-go basis, providing flexibility in purchasing software products. It offers tiered pricing based on the total number of points accumulated through purchases.

d. Server and Cloud Enrolment (SCE): SCE is designed for enterprises with significant investments in Microsoft server and cloud technologies. It provides a way to license server products, such as Windows Server or SQL Server, and cloud services like Azure, under a single agreement with simplified license management.

2. Microsoft Cloud Agreement: This agreement is specifically for enterprises that want to access Microsoft cloud services, such as Azure, Microsoft 365, or Dynamics 365. The Microsoft Cloud Agreement

outlines the terms and conditions for subscribing to and using cloud-based services. It covers topics like service availability, data protection, compliance, and usage rights.

a. Microsoft Customer Agreement: The Microsoft Customer Agreement is a standard agreement that provides a streamlined process for purchasing cloud services. It replaces the previous Microsoft Online Subscription Agreement (MOSA) and is designed to simplify the procurement of Microsoft cloud services for customers.

b. Enterprise Enrolment: The Enterprise Enrolment is an agreement designed for larger organizations that want to consolidate their cloud services under a single agreement. It allows enterprises to commit to a specific level of usage, providing flexibility, volume discounts, and additional benefits based on the enterprise's commitment.

It's important to note that the specific contracts and agreements offered by Microsoft may evolve over time, so it's recommended for enterprises to consult with Microsoft or their authorized resellers to understand the most up-to-date contract options available to them and to negotiate terms based on their specific needs and requirements.

Don't assume that the current agreements your organisation has with Microsoft are still valid. Always check for updates and changes, especially as you run up to a contract renewal.

> ***Negotiation Tip:*** *Microsoft adds/changes products, pricing and licensing rules every year, and it's not enough to think that you as you negotiated the Microsoft contract last time around, so you'll be fine again this time. Treat every Microsoft contract negotiation as a first-time event; that way you won't miss a step or make any assumptions that cost your organisation time and money down the line.*

Software Support Contracts:

Support is automatically bundled into SaaS subscriptions, so the SaaS contract (and associated monthly/annual payment) covers both license use and on-going Support.

Prior to making their software available via SaaS, Microsoft sold their software as perpetual licenses for use on a customer's premises, together with an associated Software Assurance (SA) Support Contract.

Microsoft's Software Assurance

This is a comprehensive maintenance offering that provides a range of benefits to customers who have purchased Microsoft software licenses through specific volume licensing programs, such as the Enterprise Agreement (EA) or the Enterprise Subscription Agreement (EAS). Software Assurance is an optional add-on to the licensing agreements and provides customers with a variety of valuable benefits. Let's explore what Software Assurance covers:

1. Product Upgrades and New Versions: One of the key benefits of Software Assurance is access to product upgrades and new versions of licensed software during the coverage period. This ensures that customers have the latest software releases and can take advantage of new features, improvements, and security updates.

2. Planning Services: Software Assurance includes planning services, which provide customers with access to Microsoft experts who can assist with planning and deployment of Microsoft technologies. This benefit includes consulting workshops, training sessions, and deployment planning assistance to help organizations effectively utilize Microsoft software within their IT environments.

3. Training and eLearning: Software Assurance offers training benefits that provide customers with

access to instructor-led training, online courses, and e-learning resources. These resources are designed to enhance end-user skills and technical expertise in using Microsoft software effectively. Training benefits can help organizations maximize productivity, increase user adoption, and improve overall efficiency.

4. Home Use Program (HUP): Through Software Assurance, organizations may be eligible for the Home Use Program, which allows employees to purchase discounted copies of Microsoft Office Suite or other eligible software for personal use. This benefit enables employees to have access to the same software they use at work, promoting familiarity and productivity.

5. 24x7 Problem Resolution Support: Software Assurance includes support benefits that provide organizations with 24x7 access to Microsoft technical support for product-related issues. This support can help troubleshoot and resolve software problems, ensuring minimal disruption and maximizing the value of Microsoft software investments.

6. Extended Lifecycle Support: Microsoft offers Extended Support to customers with Software Assurance for certain products that have reached the end of mainstream support. This extended coverage provides security updates, hotfixes, and technical support for a specified period beyond the standard

product lifecycle, allowing customers to maintain a secure and stable IT environment.

7. Spread Payments: For customers who opt for the Enterprise Subscription Agreement (EAS), Software Assurance offers the benefit of spreading payments for licenses and subscriptions over the subscription term, simplifying budgeting and reducing upfront costs.

It's important to note that the specific benefits and eligibility for Software Assurance may vary depending on the licensing agreement and the specific Microsoft products covered. Customers should review the terms and conditions of their Software Assurance agreement to understand the full scope of benefits available to them.

Premier Support

Microsoft's Premier Support program was a separate offering from the standard support included with Microsoft software purchases. Premier Support was a paid service that provided enhanced support and personalized assistance to larger organizations that required a higher level of technical support and proactive services to help manage complex IT environments.

It offered a range of benefits and services, including:

1. Dedicated Support: Customers were assigned a dedicated team of Microsoft support professionals who had in-depth knowledge of their specific environment and technology infrastructure.

2. Priority Access: Premier Support customers received prioritized access to Microsoft's support resources, including phone-based support, online assistance, and technical resources.

3. Proactive Services: Microsoft's Premier Support team offered proactive services to help customers optimize their IT infrastructure, identify potential issues before they become problems, and ensure smooth operations.

4. Problem Resolution: Premier Support provided assistance with troubleshooting and resolving technical issues related to Microsoft software and services, including critical incidents.

5. Knowledge Transfer: Customers could access a vast repository of technical resources, including articles, documentation, and best practices, to enhance their understanding of Microsoft technologies and improve their internal support capabilities.

6. Planning and Deployment Services: Premier Support offered guidance and assistance during the planning and deployment phases of Microsoft solutions. This helped organizations streamline their implementation processes and minimize disruptions.

7. Service Level Agreements (SLAs): Premier Support provided specific SLAs to ensure timely response and resolution of critical issues, reducing downtime and improving overall operational efficiency.

Premier Support was positioned as a high-end offering for enterprise customers.

Premier Support was replaced in late 2017 by a new offering called Unified Support.

Unified Support

Building on the services provided under the old Premier Support plan, the key features of Microsoft Unified Support include:

1. Account Management: Customers are assigned a dedicated support account manager who acts as a single point of contact for all support-related matters.

The account manager helps facilitate communications, coordinate support requests, and provide guidance on support resources.

2. Proactive Services: Microsoft Unified Support provides proactive services such as health checks, assessments, and optimization recommendations to help customers maximize the value and performance of their Microsoft technology investments.

3. Problem Resolution: Customers receive support for troubleshooting and resolving technical issues related to Microsoft software, including critical incidents. Support is typically provided through phone, online channels, and in some cases, on-site visits by Microsoft support personnel.

4. Support Planning: Microsoft Unified Support includes assistance with support planning, including reviewing support options, determining support needs, and aligning support services with the customer's IT strategy and business objectives.

5. Service Level Agreements (SLAs): Microsoft provides specific SLAs to ensure timely response and resolution of critical issues, minimizing downtime and disruption for customers.

Azure Cloud Contracts:

A Microsoft Azure Cloud contract outlines the terms and conditions of using Microsoft's Cloud services. While the specific details may vary depending on the contract and agreement between the parties involved, the main elements commonly found in an Azure Cloud contract are as follows:

1. Service Description: This section provides an overview of the Microsoft Cloud services being provided, including details on the specific services, features, and functionalities included in the agreement.

2. Service Level Agreement (SLA): This defines the performance metrics and service levels that Microsoft commits to meeting for the Cloud services. This may include uptime guarantees, response times for issue resolution, and compensation provisions in case of service-level breaches.

3. Scope of Use: Outlines the permitted use of the Microsoft Cloud services, including any restrictions on usage, user limits, and the scope of the licensed software or services.

4. Data Security and Privacy: This part addresses the measures taken by Microsoft to ensure the security and privacy of customer data stored or processed in the Cloud. It may include provisions

related to data encryption, data access controls, data retention, and compliance with applicable data protection regulations.

5. Intellectual Property Rights: This clarifies the ownership and intellectual property rights associated with the Cloud services, including any licensing terms and restrictions.

6. Support Services: This section outlines the Support services provided by Microsoft for the Cloud services, including technical support, issue resolution procedures, and support channels.

7. Pricing and Payment Terms: This includes details on the pricing structure for the cloud services, including subscription fees, usage-based charges, and any additional fees or costs. It also specifies the payment terms and any applicable terms for price changes or discounts.

8. Term and Termination: This part defines the duration of the contract, including the start and end dates, and any automatic renewal provisions. It also outlines the conditions and procedures for terminating the agreement, including notice periods and any termination fees.

9. Liability and Indemnification: This addresses the allocation of liability between the parties and any indemnification provisions. It may include limitations

of liability, disclaimers, and obligations to indemnify each other against certain claims or damages.

10. Confidentiality: This section outlines the obligations of both parties to maintain the confidentiality of information shared during the course of the agreement.

11. Governing Law and Dispute Resolution: This section specifies the governing law that will apply to the contract and the procedures for resolving any disputes or claims that may arise.

It's important to note that the specific terms and conditions of an Azure Cloud contract may vary based on the type of Cloud services, the customer's unique requirements, and any negotiated terms during the contracting process. It's advisable to review the contract carefully and consult with Microsoft representatives or your own legal professionals for a comprehensive understanding of the specific terms and conditions.

Services Contracts:

A Microsoft Services contract typically includes several key elements that outline the terms and conditions of engaging Microsoft's Services for implementation, customization, or consulting purposes. While the specific details may vary depending on the contract and agreement between the parties involved, the main elements commonly found in a Microsoft Services contract are as follows:

1. Scope of Services: This section defines the specific services to be provided by Microsoft, including implementation, customization, consulting, training, or other professional services. It outlines the goals, deliverables, and timelines for the engagement.

2. Project Plan and Milestones: This includes a detailed project plan that outlines the tasks, milestones, and timelines associated with the services engagement. It may specify the responsibilities of both parties and the project management approach.

3. Resources and Personnel: This part specifies the resources allocated by Microsoft to the engagement, including the qualifications and expertise of the personnel who will be providing the services. It may include the roles and responsibilities of key individuals involved in the project.

4. Change Management: This addresses the process for handling any changes or modifications to the scope, timeline, or deliverables of the engagement. It may include provisions for change orders, change request procedures, and associated costs or adjustments.

5. Acceptance Criteria: This section outlines the criteria and procedures for accepting or rejecting the deliverables or milestones of the engagement. It may include testing, validation, or acceptance procedures to ensure the satisfactory completion of the services.

6. Fees and Payment Terms: This includes details on the fees or pricing structure for the services engagement, including hourly rates, fixed fees, or other payment arrangements. It specifies the payment terms, invoicing schedule, and any additional costs or expenses that may be incurred.

7. Intellectual Property Rights: This clarifies the ownership and intellectual property rights associated with any deliverables or work products created during the engagement. It may include provisions related to licensing, use, and restrictions on the use of the deliverables.

8. Confidentiality: This section outlines the obligations of both parties to maintain the confidentiality of proprietary or sensitive information

shared during the engagement. It may include non-disclosure agreements or confidentiality provisions.

9. Limitation of Liability: This addresses the allocation of liability between the parties and any limitations or exclusions of liability for damages or losses arising from the services engagement.

10. Termination: This part defines the conditions and procedures for terminating the services engagement. It may include provisions related to termination for convenience, termination for cause, notice periods, and any associated termination fees or obligations.

11. Governing Law and Dispute Resolution: This specifies the governing law that will apply to the contract and the procedures for resolving any disputes or claims that may arise from the services engagement.

It's important to note that the specific terms and conditions of a Microsoft Services contract may vary based on the nature of the services, the customer's unique requirements, and any negotiated terms during the contracting process. It's advisable to review the contract carefully and consult with Microsoft representatives or your own legal professionals for a comprehensive understanding of the specific terms and conditions.

Negotiation Tip: *it's well worth taking your time to understand all the various agreements Microsoft offers, and to then communicate widely within your organisation once paperwork has been signed to ensure everyone stays compliant with what has been agreed. Too many companies sign a Microsoft deal and then either by accident or forgetfulness they then don't strictly adhere to the software licencing conditions and soon find themselves later subjected to an expensive and embarrassing software audit by Microsoft.*

Chapter 5

Negotiation Preparation

Do Your Homework:

Knowledge is power. You can't expect to negotiate a great deal with Microsoft (or any supplier) if you aren't fully prepared.

Rest assured, your Microsoft sales rep will have been preparing and planning your contract negotiation well in advance and will have been monitoring your license usage. The sales rep will have also been encouraging your users to evaluate new Microsoft products and services to see if there is opportunity to expand the existing Microsoft footprint and grow revenues.

So a good buyer will also have done their homework to fully understand what Microsoft products and services their organisation has got today, and what it will likely need in the next three years. And all of this should be done before any meetings take place about any new deal or renewal with the Microsoft sales rep.

It's likely that software use and business requirements will have changed since your last Microsoft agreement was signed. Perhaps your organization has more or fewer users. Maybe what you bought before might no longer be fit for purpose. Maybe your company has new software needs or requirements that Microsoft could also help with.

> **Negotiating Tip:** *Negotiating with Microsoft is not easy so it's key to start preparing and planning early, e.g., commence this work at least six months prior to your Microsoft contract renewal date. Don't leave it too late as last-minute deals leave all the negotiation power in the hands of Microsoft and you'll likely end up paying far more than you need to, and maybe even end up buying more stuff than you want too!*

Key Elements To Consider:

Preparing for a negotiation with Microsoft will help a company navigate the process more effectively and increase the chances of securing favourable terms and pricing.

Here are some key steps to consider when preparing for a negotiation with Microsoft:

1. Understand Your Requirements: Clearly define your organization's current and future requirements, including the specific Microsoft software products or

services needed, the expected usage, deployment scope, and any customization or support requirements.

2. Have a solid understanding of your timelines and budget constraints.

3. Research Microsoft's offerings: Conduct thorough research on the Microsoft products and services you are interested in. Understand their features, licensing metrics, and pricing models. Look at their product roadmaps and see what's coming that might also be of interest to you. This knowledge will help you to have informed discussions with Microsoft during the negotiation.

4. Establish a Negotiation Team: Assemble a negotiation team comprising individuals with the necessary expertise, including IT professionals, procurement specialists, legal counsel, and financial representatives. Ensure they are well-versed in the company's requirements and are prepared to advocate for your organization's interests during the negotiation.

5. Set Clear Objectives and Priorities: Define your negotiation objectives and priorities. Determine the key terms and conditions that are crucial to your organization's success, such as pricing, licensing metrics, support, maintenance, or contractual flexibility. Identify potential areas where you may be

willing to compromise and those where you need to stand firm.

6.   Gather Market Intelligence: Research market trends and industry benchmarks. This insight may well uncover negotiation leverage you can use to your advantage during the negotiation process.

7.   Consider External Expertise: If necessary, consult with external experts or consultants who have experience negotiating with Microsoft. They can provide valuable insights, strategies, and guidance throughout the negotiation process to help you better achieve an optimal outcome.

8.   Competitive Pressure: Microsoft has several competitors in the software and cloud markets and in the right circumstances these can provide negotiation leverage:

- Google offers a range of cloud-based services including databases, analytics, and machine learning that compete with Microsoft's cloud offerings. Google also offers its own Office applications that compete with Microsoft's Office 365 suite.

- Oracle offers a wide range of software products including database and applications that compete with Microsoft's database and business applications, and Oracle cloud is a competitive player in the Cloud space.

- SAP is a leading provider of enterprise software solutions for business operations, customer relationship management, and supply chain management that competes with Microsoft's applications. As does SAP's flagship database product HANA.

- Salesforce is a cloud-based software provider that offers customer relationship management (CRM) and other business applications that compete with many of Microsoft's SaaS cloud offerings.

- Amazon Web Services: AWS offers a range of cloud-based services including IaaS, PaaS, databases, analytics, and machine learning that compete with Microsoft's cloud offerings.

Overall, Microsoft faces competition from several major players in the software industry and in certain circumstances this can create strong negotiation leverage for an organisation negotiating with Microsoft.

Microsoft's Sales Process

Microsoft's sales process typically involves several stages and interactions between Microsoft sales representatives and their customers.

Here is a general overview of Microsoft's sales process:

1. Initial Contact and Discovery: The process usually begins with the customer making initial contact with Microsoft, either by reaching out directly or through Microsoft's marketing channels. At this stage, Microsoft sales reps engage in discovery conversations to understand the customer's business needs, challenges, and objectives. They gather information to determine the most relevant Microsoft solutions and services that can address the customer's requirements. If it's a Microsoft contract renewal, they will be looking to grow the revenues from each customer at every renewal, and so the Microsoft sales rep will be on the hunt to cross-sell into new departments or divisions of the client, and/or upsell to add more products/services to grow the Microsoft footprint.

2. Solution Presentation and Proposal: Based on the gathered information, Microsoft sales reps create a tailored solution presentation and proposal. They showcase Microsoft's products, services, and technologies that align with the customer's needs. The

proposal may include details on software licensing options, implementation services, support offerings, and pricing estimates.

3. Solution Demonstration and Proof of Concept (POC): If it's a new opportunity, Microsoft may provide demonstrations or proof of concept to showcase the capabilities of their solutions. This could involve providing access to software trials or conducting live demonstrations tailored to the customer's specific use cases. The goal is to give the customer a hands-on experience and validate the solution's fit for their requirements.

4. Contract Negotiation and Pricing Discussion: Once the customer expresses interest in moving forward, the negotiation stage begins. Microsoft sales reps work with the customer to refine the solution, address any concerns or questions, and negotiate the contract terms. This includes discussing licensing metrics, pricing, payment terms, support agreements, and any customization or specific requirements.

5. Contract Finalization and Approval: Once both parties reach an agreement on the contract terms, the contract can be finalized and signed.

6. Implementation and Deployment Planning: After the contract is signed, the customer and Microsoft collaborate to plan the implementation and deployment process. This may involve scoping the

project, assigning resources, defining timelines, and determining any necessary integration or customization requirements.

7. Deployment and Support: The implementation and deployment phase will commence with Microsoft's Services team (or a Microsoft Partner) working closely with the customer to deploy the software, configure the system, migrate data, and provide training.

8. Ongoing Relationship and Account Management: Once the software is deployed, Microsoft maintains an ongoing relationship with the customer. Account managers and customer success teams provide support, monitor customer satisfaction, and explore future opportunities for upselling, cross-selling, or expanding the usage of Microsoft products and services based on the customer's evolving needs.

It's important to note that each customer situation is different, so Microsoft's sales process may have variations or additional steps depending on the specific product, industry, or customer requirements.

Managing Your Microsoft Sales Rep

Managing and controlling a Microsoft sales rep requires proactive engagement and clear communication.

The Microsoft sales rep has a high sales target to meet and is very well compensated and rewarded for making and exceeding that target. So your deal, especially if it's a large deal, will be critical to their sales plans this year.

Here are some steps that a buyer can take to effectively manage and control interactions with a Microsoft sales rep:

1. Clearly Define Requirements: Before engaging with the Microsoft sales rep, clearly define your organization's requirements, including the specific needs, objectives, and constraints. This should also include informing the sales rep about how you expect communication with your organisation to occur during the negotiation process. You don't want the sales rep talking to everyone in your organisation; you want the information flow controlled and directed via your negotiation lead at all times in order to avoid missteps or misunderstandings. This will help you maintain focus during discussions and ensure that the sales rep understands your priorities.

2.   Conduct Market Research: Conduct thorough market research to gain a solid understanding of Microsoft's products, pricing models, and competitive offerings. This knowledge will empower you to ask informed questions and evaluate the sales rep's proposals effectively.

3.   Establish Clear Objectives: Set clear objectives and criteria that you expect the Microsoft sales rep to meet. Clearly communicate your expectations regarding transparency on pricing, licensing, support, implementation, and other key factors. This will help align the sales rep's efforts with your requirements.

4.   Ask for Multiple Options: Request multiple options or scenarios from the Microsoft sales rep, including different pricing models, licensing metrics, support levels, and implementation approaches. This will enable you to compare and evaluate different proposals to find the best fit for your organization.

5.   Request Documentation: Ask for detailed documentation of the proposed solution, including licensing terms, service-level agreements (SLAs), and contractual terms. Review these documents carefully to ensure they align with your requirements and are reasonable and fair.

6.   Involve Internal Stakeholders: Engage relevant stakeholders within your organization, such as IT professionals, legal counsel, finance and procurement

specialists, during the negotiation process. Their expertise and input can help evaluate proposals, ensure compliance, and provide valuable insights.

7. Request Clarifications: If any aspect of the sales rep's proposal or documentation is unclear or requires further explanation, don't hesitate to seek clarification. Ask specific questions to gain a better understanding and ensure that you are making informed decisions.

8. Negotiate and Seek Concessions: Engage in negotiation with the Microsoft sales rep to seek concessions that align with your objectives. Negotiate pricing, licensing metrics, support terms, and any other contractual terms that require adjustment to better suit your needs. Be prepared to push back on unreasonable terms or costs.

9. Document Agreements in Writing: Ensure that all agreements and changes made during the negotiation are documented in writing. This can help avoid misunderstandings or disputes later on. Keep a record of all correspondence, proposals, and contractual documents exchanged during the process.

10. Maintain Regular Communication: Maintain open and regular communication with the Microsoft sales rep throughout the engagement. Clearly communicate your expectations, provide feedback, and address any concerns promptly. Regular

communication helps maintain transparency and ensures that everyone remains aligned.

Remember, managing and controlling a Microsoft sales representative requires active participation, clear communication, and a well-defined understanding of your organization's needs and priorities. By following these steps, you can effectively manage the sales process and drive outcomes that best suit your requirements.

> **Negotiation Tip:** There can be significant benefit in trying to get to know your Microsoft Sales rep as that can uncover their personal motivation and objectives for the up-coming deal. Such collaboration can often help create a better deal that works for them and for you, so always explore this with them. Ask how they will be compensated and what's important to them about any new or renewal deal you do.

Chapter 6

Negotiating Paperwork

<u>Always Take Legal Advice:</u>

Like most Technology vendors, Microsoft's contracts are complex and have many nuances which need to be legally reviewed and thoroughly understood prior to signing.

When looking at Microsoft's paperwork, always take legal advice, either from your organisation's in-house company lawyers, or if your company doesn't have in-house lawyers then buy external legal advice from lawyers who specialise in software licensing.

From a negotiation perspective, Microsoft will likely resist any requests for changes to their contract language as they want to keep things simple and consistent across their whole customer base. That means negotiating changes to Microsoft contract terms and conditions is tough. But it is possible.

Some items Microsoft will change and some they won't. The key here is - if you don't ask you don't get. If your legal counsel wants to see change in a standard clause in one of Microsoft's contracts then put that to Microsoft and make it part of your negotiation.

Explain clearly why the change is important for your organisation.

> **Negotiation Tip:** Microsoft may still say 'no' to some of the contractual changes you request. But maybe you can accept that as it will at least give you a bargaining chip as a potential trade-off for something else that you really do want to get out of the negotiation. For example, you may ask for 90-day payment terms and Microsoft says 'no'. Then in return you can say 'so if we can't have 90-day payment terms, what else can Microsoft offer to sweeten the deal financially, e.g. how about quarterly billing instead of annual billing?'

Microsoft Software Contracts:

When negotiating a Microsoft software contract, the terms and conditions should be carefully considered and potentially negotiated to better align with your organization's needs and to protect its interests.

While the specific terms and conditions you might want changed will vary based on your organisation's particular requirements, here are some key contractual terms and conditions you should ensure you review during the negotiation:

1. Licensing Metrics: Review and discuss the licensing metrics that best suit your usage patterns and requirements. Consider factors such as User profiles (e.g., a warehouse user may be fine with an E1 Office 365 license, but head office workers will need either E3, F3 or E5 licenses). Ensure the chosen licensing metric aligns with your organization's current and future needs.

2. Support and Maintenance: Address the terms and level of support and maintenance provided by Microsoft. Discuss response times, availability, escalation procedures, and service-level agreements (SLAs). Seek clarity on any additional fees or costs associated with Premium or Unified support levels.

3. Customization and Integration: If customization or integration with other systems is required, negotiate the terms and scope of such services. Ensure the contract clearly defines the responsibilities, deliverables, timelines, and associated costs for customization or integration projects.

4. Data Security and Privacy: Discuss data security and privacy requirements, including compliance with applicable data protection laws and regulations. Seek assurance that Microsoft will handle your

organization's data appropriately and implement necessary security measures.

5. Subscription Flexibility: Request flexibility that allows you to shift spend between products in the same Ordering Document. This will help optimise your spend and avoid having to subscribe for extra licences as your needs change.

6. Termination and Renewal: Review the termination and renewal clauses. Pay particular attention to notice periods, conditions for termination or non-renewal, and associated costs or penalties. Consider negotiating more favourable renewal terms, such as pricing caps or discounted renewal rates.

7. Audit and Compliance: Clarify Microsoft's audit procedures and any compliance requirements. Understand your rights and responsibilities in case of an audit, including reporting and license management obligations. Seek clarity on how Microsoft handles license compliance and any potential financial implications.

8. Intellectual Property Rights: Address the ownership and use of intellectual property rights related to the software or any customizations created during the engagement. Ensure the contract clearly defines the rights and limitations on the use, modification, and distribution of the software and associated intellectual property.

9. Liability and Indemnification: Discuss the allocation of liability between the parties and any limitations or exclusions of liability. Seek reasonable limits on liability and ensure appropriate indemnification provisions are in place to protect your organization from claims or damages.

10. Transition Services: This is key if you want to have some flexibility built into the contract that allows you to move from Microsoft to another software or services supplier at some point in the future. There should be some form of provision that states what Microsoft will do if your organisation chooses to leave Microsoft and you want your data transferred to your new supplier.

11. Mergers, Acquisitions and Divestments: Be clear about what happens to your contract and contracted spend when a significant event occurs such as a merger, an acquisition or a divestment. Without careful consideration of such future events, you may find you can't cancel the contract or amend it without financial penalty.

12. Dispute Resolution: Consider the dispute resolution mechanisms outlined in the contract. Evaluate whether alternative dispute resolution methods, such as mediation or arbitration, are suitable for your organization's needs. Seek a fair and balanced approach to resolving potential disputes.

It's important to review all of Microsoft's contracts comprehensively and to consider whether there are any other specific terms that may be relevant to your organization's circumstances or industry requirements.

Microsoft Cloud Contracts:

When negotiating a Microsoft Cloud contract, there are several key items that should be carefully considered and potentially negotiated to align with your organization's needs.

Apart from negotiating cloud pricing which is covered later in this book, here are the main contractual areas to focus on when negotiating an Microsoft Cloud contract:

1. Service Scope and Level: Clearly define the scope of the cloud services being provided, including specific services, features, and functionalities. Discuss and negotiate the service level agreements (SLAs) that govern the performance, availability, and reliability of the cloud services.

2. Data Security and Privacy: Address data security and privacy requirements. Discuss the

measures Microsoft has in place to ensure the security and confidentiality of your data. Negotiate contractual terms that align with your organization's data protection policies and compliance requirements.

3. Service Level Agreements (SLAs): Negotiate SLAs that align with your organization's needs and expectations. Discuss performance targets, uptime guarantees, response times for issue resolution, and compensation provisions in case of service-level breaches.

4. Compliance and Regulatory Requirements: Address any specific compliance or regulatory requirements that your organization needs to adhere to, such as industry-specific regulations or data protection laws. Ensure that the cloud services provided by Microsoft comply with these requirements.

5. Data Ownership and Portability: Clarify data ownership rights and negotiate provisions that allow you to retain ownership of your data stored or processed in the Microsoft Cloud. Discuss data portability options to ensure you can easily extract and move your data if needed.

6. Termination and Exit Strategy: Negotiate termination provisions, including notice periods, conditions, and any associated costs or penalties for terminating the contract. Define the process for

transitioning out of the Microsoft Cloud and retrieving your data at the end of the agreement term.

7. Support and Maintenance: Discuss the support services provided by Microsoft for the cloud services. Clarify any additional support offerings or premium services available.

8. Disaster Recovery and Business Continuity: Address disaster recovery and business continuity measures provided by Microsoft. Discuss recovery time objectives (RTOs) and recovery point objectives (RPOs) and negotiate appropriate levels of redundancy and backup procedures to meet your organization's needs.

9. Intellectual Property Rights: Clarify the ownership and use of intellectual property rights associated with the cloud services. Negotiate clear terms that define your rights, limitations, and restrictions on the use, modification, and distribution of any intellectual property created or utilized within the Microsoft Cloud environment.

10. Liability and Indemnification: Discuss the allocation of liability between the parties and any limitations or exclusions of liability for damages or losses. Negotiate provisions that protect your organization's interests and include appropriate indemnification provisions.

11. Dispute Resolution: Consider the dispute resolution mechanisms outlined in the cloud contract. Evaluate whether alternative dispute resolution methods, such as mediation or arbitration, are suitable for your organization's needs. Seek a fair and efficient process for resolving any potential disputes that may arise.

Engaging legal counsel or experts who specialize in cloud contracts can provide valuable insights and guidance throughout the negotiation process. They can help ensure that the Microsoft Cloud contract protects your organization's interests, complies with applicable laws and regulations, and provides the flexibility and value you seek.

Microsoft Services Contracts:

When looking to buy Microsoft Services or Consulting, there are several key items that you should consider and potentially negotiate to ensure a favourable agreement that aligns with your organization's needs.

Here are the main contractual items to focus on when negotiating Microsoft Services:

1. Scope of Services: Clearly define the scope of the services you require from Microsoft's Services and Consulting. Identify the specific services, deliverables, and outcomes you expect from the engagement. Discuss and negotiate the scope to ensure it aligns with your project objectives.

2. Service Level Agreements (SLAs): Negotiate service level agreements that govern the performance, responsiveness, and quality of the services. Define metrics, such as response times, project milestones, and deliverable timelines, and include provisions for penalties or remedies in case of SLA breaches.

3. Resource Allocation and Expertise: Discuss and negotiate the resources assigned to your project, including the expertise, experience, and qualifications of the consultants or team members who will be working on your engagement. Ensure that the team has the necessary skills and knowledge to meet your specific requirements.

4. Project Management and Communication: Address the project management approach, communication channels, and reporting mechanisms. Clarify the frequency and format of project updates, progress reports, and stakeholder involvement. Ensure that there is effective communication and collaboration throughout the engagement.

5. Pricing and Payment Terms: Negotiate the pricing structure for the services. Discuss the billing rates, payment milestones, and any additional fees or expenses associated with the engagement. Seek clarity on the cost of any optional or additional services that may be required.

6. Intellectual Property Rights: Clarify the ownership and use of intellectual property rights associated with the services and deliverables. Discuss any licensing or usage rights granted to your organization and negotiate provisions that protect your intellectual property rights and ensure appropriate usage restrictions.

7. Confidentiality and Data Security: Discuss and negotiate confidentiality and data security provisions to protect your organization's sensitive information. Address data privacy, protection, and compliance requirements. Ensure that Microsoft's staff and consultants adhere to your organization's data security policies and industry regulations.

8. Change Management and Flexibility: Address change management procedures, including the ability to accommodate changes in project scope, timelines, or deliverables. Discuss how changes will be handled, including any impact on pricing or timelines. Seek flexibility to adjust the project as needed throughout the engagement.

9. Acceptance Criteria and Sign-Off: Establish acceptance criteria and sign-off procedures for each deliverable or milestone. Define the process for reviewing, evaluating, and approving the work performed by Microsoft's staff or consultants. Ensure that acceptance criteria are well-defined and realistic.

10. Liability and Indemnification: Discuss the allocation of liability between the parties and any limitations or exclusions of liability for damages or losses. Negotiate provisions that protect your organization's interests and include appropriate indemnification provisions.

11. Termination and Transition: Address termination provisions, including notice periods, conditions, and any associated costs or penalties for terminating the contract. Define the process for transitioning the project to your organization or to another service provider, if necessary.

12. Dispute Resolution: Consider the dispute resolution mechanisms outlined in the contract. Evaluate whether alternative dispute resolution methods, such as mediation or arbitration, are suitable for your organization's needs. Seek a fair and efficient process for resolving any potential disputes that may arise.

Engaging legal counsel and experts who specialize in professional services contracts can provide valuable insights and guidance throughout the negotiation process. They can help ensure that the contract protects your organization's interests, complies with applicable laws and regulations, and provides the flexibility and value you seek.

Chapter 7

Negotiating Software Pricing

Discount Options:

Companies can negotiate various discounts for Microsoft software licenses based on factors such as the volume of licenses being purchased, the length of the contract term, the specific products being purchased, their historic discount level, and the level of support services required.

Some of the discounts that companies can negotiate for Microsoft software include:

1. Volume discounts: Companies that purchase a large number of licenses can negotiate lower prices per license. As standard, Microsoft offers four bands of volume discount (A, B, C and D) as follows:

Discount Level	Number of Users or Devices
A	500 – 2399
B	2400 – 5999
C	6000 – 14999
D	15000+

> **Negotiation Tip:** Some customers think that when Microsoft applies an ABCD volume discount then that's the end of the price negotiation. That's a mistake! Once the ABCD volume discount has been applied, then that should be seen as just the start of the price negotiation. For example, if a customer had 7000 users then they would get Level C volume discount applied automatically. The customer should then view this Level C price as their starting point for further negotiation and should be aiming to get more discount applied to any final deal.

2. Term discounts: Companies that agree to a longer contract term can sometimes negotiate a better discount on the total cost of the contract.

3. Bundled discounts: Companies that purchase multiple Microsoft products as a bundle can often negotiate a discount so that the bundle costs less than the sum of the parts of that bundle. For example, Microsoft might be keen to promote a new product (or conversely one that's not selling well) so it will bundle it with another product or products to try to boost sales of the new (or lagging) product.

4. Upgrade discounts: Companies that upgrade from older versions of Microsoft software can sometimes negotiate a discount on the new licenses.

Discounts can also vary by product. For example, Microsoft offers various licensing programs for Office 365, including Enterprise Agreement (EA), Enterprise Agreement Subscription (EAS), Microsoft Products and Services Agreement (MPSA), and Cloud Solution Provider (CSP). These programs have different pricing structures and discount models.

In general, larger enterprises that purchase a significant number of licenses or commit to long-term agreements with Microsoft can often negotiate better discounts. Volume licensing typically offers higher discounts compared to individual or retail purchases. Additionally, some organizations may qualify for special pricing based on their status as educational institutions or non-profit organizations.

It's important to note that the specific discount ranges are not publicly disclosed by Microsoft and can vary based on the individual circumstances of each enterprise. To determine the exact range of discounts available, it is recommended you contact Microsoft or authorized resellers or independent Consultants with experience of negotiating Microsoft software contracts directly and discuss your organization's specific requirements and negotiation options.

> **Negotiation Tip:** *Whatever mix of products or services you buy from Microsoft, they will often initially produce proposals or quotes that simply show a list of items and then one total net cost. This is commonly referred to as 'price bundling'. There are no list prices shown, there is no explanation as to how the net price has been arrived at, and there is no way to see how discounting has been applied. The first step for any negotiator is to demand that Microsoft unbundle their pricing so that it is clear, line by line and product by product, what the list price of each product is and what discounts have been applied to each line item. This can reveal discount variation from one item to the next which can be challenged at the negotiation table.*

Negotiating Trade-in Credits:

If you are a Microsoft customer that is still using their older legacy perpetual licences and are considering moving to any of their SaaS products, then as part of the negotiation you should demand a trade-in credit on the legacy perpetual licenses to help offset the price of the new SaaS software. Microsoft are open to such negotiation tactics and depending on the size and timing of your deal you may find they are quite generous when it comes to credit applied in order to encourage you to move to their SaaS products. Especially if that move to SaaS includes a move to Microsoft Azure Cloud too.

Note: for European customers of Microsoft that still use on-premises legacy perpetual licenses, then there is a market for 'used' pre-owned Microsoft licenses. Validated by the European Union courts, and only available in Europe, Microsoft's European customers can leverage this in two ways:

1. If a Microsoft customer is looking to upgrade to Office 365 SaaS, then the customer can help fund some of that migration by selling their 'pre-owned' Microsoft on-premise perpetual licenses to a Microsoft Broker.

2. Alternatively, the customer could get a price from a Broker and then ask Microsoft to offer a better trade-in price. Microsoft is keen to reduce the amount of pre-owned licenses available via Brokers and so may well offer the customer a better trade-in price!

> **Negotiation Tip:** *Be aware that when negotiating any renewal, Microsoft looks at each deal separately and is often loath to consider total historic spend. You may have got a good discount on your last Microsoft deal, but that discount likely won't carry forward to your next Microsoft deal. The discount offered on your next deal will simply be based on the size of that new deal. So either consolidate buying to make the spend pot as big as you can each time, or look to renegotiate and consolidate contracts to have more spend on the negotiating table at the same time in order to influence Microsoft to discount more.*

Negotiating True Ups and True Downs

A "True-up" refers to the process of reconciling the number of software licenses a customer has deployed with the number of licenses they have purchased. It is an important part of Microsoft's license compliance and auditing procedures.

During a True-up, a customer is required to report their current software usage to Microsoft, typically on an annual basis or at the end of a specified licensing period. The customer provides details about the software products they have deployed, the number of licenses they own, and any changes or additions made since the previous reporting period.

The purpose of a True-up is to ensure that the customer is properly licensed for the Microsoft software they are using. If there is a discrepancy between the number of licenses owned and the number of software installations or users, the customer may need to acquire additional licenses to achieve compliance.

The True-up process helps Microsoft and the customer maintain compliance with licensing agreements and ensures that the customer has the appropriate licenses to cover their software usage. It is a way for organizations to regularly assess their licensing needs, make any necessary adjustments, and ensure ongoing compliance with Microsoft's licensing terms and conditions.

It's worth noting that the specific details and procedures of a True-up can vary depending on the licensing agreements and terms negotiated between Microsoft and the customer. It is recommended to consult the licensing documentation or reach out to Microsoft directly for accurate information on the True-up process specific to your organization.

A 'True Down' is not a formal Microsoft term as they don't like to see clients reduce their Microsoft estate or spend levels. Customers whose user counts reduced due to their organisation shrinking were often frustrated to find that there was no mechanism in Microsoft's standard agreements to cater for a reduction in workforce and so a pro rata reduction of Microsoft's licenses and fees.

In effect, when a customer signs an Enterprise Agreement (EA), the number of users/licenses stated at the start of the EA term was a hard baseline of users/licenses and Microsoft expected to see that level of spend remain flat (at worst) through the three-year term, or to see the level of spend grow (at best) as the client's organisation grew. That's good for Microsoft, but not so good for customers who want complete flexibility to increase or decrease their license count and associated spend.

> ***Negotiation Tip:*** *A key element of any Microsoft negotiation is to obtain some form of 'True Down' facility in the EA to cater for workforce and license reductions. For example, some words to the effect of 'should the customer's workforce reduce by 10% or more during the EA term, then Microsoft would adjust the future license count and spend accordingly'.*

Chapter 8

Negotiating Support Costs

Microsoft Support

As a quick reminder, Microsoft support covers such essential items as technical support, access to software updates, bug fixes, patches, and security updates. This base level of support is included as standard in all product licenses and as part of the Enterprise Agreement (EA).

Software Assurance (SA)

For older legacy on-premises perpetual use licenses, upgrade rights and enhanced support was provided via a separate contract called Software Assurance.

Customers with SA pay an annual fee of 25% of the volume license fee for server products and 29% for desktop products.

Negotiating SA costs for Microsoft's perpetual licenses can be a complex process, but here are some steps that a business can take to navigate the negotiation process:

1. Understand your current SA agreement: Review the terms, coverage, and pricing. This will help you identify areas where you may have leverage or opportunities for cost reduction.

2. Evaluate your Support needs: Assess your actual support requirements based on your usage, criticality of systems, and business needs. Determine if you are utilizing all the features and services included in your current SA agreement, as this can impact the cost negotiations.

3. Identify areas for cost reduction: This could include consolidating licenses, reducing Support levels for certain products or systems that are less critical, or bundling SA services with other purchases.

4. Build a business case: Develop a strong business case that outlines the reasons for requesting lower SA costs. This could include factors such as financial constraints, competitive pricing from other vendors or third parties, or reduced SA requirements due to system changes or upgrades.

5. Leverage your relationship: If you have a long-standing relationship with Microsoft, emphasize the long-term value you bring as a customer and the potential for future business. Highlight any positive experiences, references, or referrals that can strengthen your negotiating position.

> **Negotiation Tip:** In the past, some Microsoft customers terminated their SA agreements to avoid the costs of SA. They evaluated their use of Microsoft products and determined that they were happy with the current versions of the software they had and were not interested in upgrading to any newer versions in the next three or more years. This saved them a lot of money. They found it was cheaper to avoid SA, sweat their existing Microsoft assets for several years, and then re-purchase a whole new set of the latest Microsoft products at some future date. This frustrated Microsoft no end as they lost out on a lot of SA revenues. The advent of SaaS, which comes pre-bundled with SA features as standard, removed this 'drop SA' option for customers, much to the delight of Microsoft!

Support Costs for SaaS

Microsoft SaaS applications are sold as a subscription bundle as that fee covers both software licenses as well as associated support and upgrade rights.

Unified Support

Microsoft reps will tell you that Unified Support is necessary because the Microsoft support that comes as standard with each licensed product, and that's included as standard within your Enterprise Agreement (EA), is only baseline support. As a result, the rep will likely tell you that your organisation needs Unified Support if it wants to enjoy better quality support with faster response times. But Unified does come at a premium price and not all companies need this extra level of support.

Unified Support fees are based on a percentage of your organization's existing spend with Microsoft.

Unified pricing starts at 6% of Office 365 and client software annual costs, and 8% of other software and online services annual costs for the entry point service.

It then rises to 10% of Office 365 and client software annual costs, and 12% of other software and online services annual costs for the premium version.

Legacy Premier Support agreements would clearly outline the hours, services, and resources that you were entitled to. Unified Support offers 'unlimited support' and as a result its fees are higher than Premier Support was. Based on this model, it's easy to see how escalating Microsoft user, server and Azure fees lead to an increased Unified Support cost as well, which is good for Microsoft and their revenues, but not so good for the customer who sees their Unified costs rising year after year.

Negotiating Microsoft's Unified Support, or any support agreement, requires careful preparation and an understanding of your organization's specific needs and goals.

Here are some steps to consider when negotiating a Unified support agreement with Microsoft:

1. Assess your needs: Before entering into negotiations, assess your organization's support requirements. Identify the Microsoft products and services you use, the level of support you need (e.g., 24/7 availability, response times), and any specific business-critical or custom requirements. You may well find that you're your organisation doesn't need the premium services provided by Unified support and that the standard support provided as part of your EA agreement is more than sufficient. Unified support appeals most to larger enterprises with more complex support needs.

2. Research Microsoft's offerings: Familiarize yourself with Microsoft's Unified support offerings, including the available tiers, features, and pricing structures. Microsoft's website and support documentation are good starting points for understanding their support options.

3. Define your objectives: Determine your negotiation objectives and prioritize them. For example, you may want to achieve cost savings, obtain additional support services, or tailor the agreement to meet your specific needs. Having clear objectives will help guide your negotiation strategy.

4. Leverage your existing relationship: Highlight your organization's commitment to Microsoft products and services over many years and emphasize the potential for long-term partnership if a reasonably priced Unified support agreement can be agreed.

5. Request customized solutions: Don't be afraid to request customized solutions or modifications to the standard Unified support offerings. This may include adjusting service levels, tailoring response times, or including additional services to align with your specific requirements.

6. Discuss pricing and terms: Clarify the pricing and terms of the Unified support agreement. Demand transparency on how the Unified pricing proposed by Microsoft has been calculated across each element of Microsoft expenditure including products and Azure. Explore potential discounts or incentives based on your organization's size or usage and consider options for multi-year agreements that may offer better cost savings.

7. Review the contract: Carefully review the proposed Unified support agreement, paying particular attention to terms and conditions, service level agreements (SLAs), renewal policies, and any limitations or exclusions. Ensure that the final contract aligns with the negotiated terms you have agreed and meets your organization's specific requirements.

8. Seek legal and technical input: Involve legal and technical experts within your organization to review the contract and provide insights into any potential legal or technical implications. Their input can help ensure that the agreement is comprehensive and satisfactory.

9. Consider alternatives: If the negotiated terms are not meeting your objectives, consider alternative support options. Microsoft's Partners or independent third parties may have other support programs or offerings that could better align with your needs at a more cost-effective price point.

Chapter 9

Negotiating Cloud Costs

Factors that affect Azure cloud pricing

Microsoft Azure cloud services are priced based on a consumption-based model, where you pay for the resources and services you utilize. The pricing structure for Azure can be complex, as it involves various factors such as the specific services you use, the quantity of resources consumed, and any additional features or support options.

Here are some key factors that can impact the pricing of Microsoft Azure:

1. Resource Usage: Azure services are billed based on the quantity and type of resources you consume, such as virtual machines, storage, networking, and data transfers. The pricing is typically based on an hourly or monthly rate, depending on the service.

2. Service Tiers: Azure offers different service tiers for certain services, providing varying performance levels, scalability options, and features. The pricing may differ based on the chosen tier.

3. Reserved Instances: Azure provides the option to purchase Reserved Instances, which allow you to

commit to a specific resource for a predetermined period, such as one or three years. This commitment can lead to cost savings compared to on-demand pricing.

4. Pricing Calculator: Microsoft offers an Azure Pricing Calculator that allows you to estimate the costs based on your resource usage and service selections. The calculator takes into account various factors, such as region, instance type, storage size, and data transfer volume.

5. Discounts and Offers: Microsoft periodically offers discounts, promotions, and special pricing for specific services or scenarios. These can include options like Azure Hybrid Benefit, which provides cost savings for customers with existing on-premises licenses.

6. Support Options: Azure offers different support plans, such as Basic, Developer, Standard, and Professional Direct, which provide varying levels of technical support. The support plans have associated costs depending on the level of assistance required.

7. Enterprise Agreements: For larger organizations, Microsoft may offer customized pricing through Enterprise Agreements (EA) and Server and Cloud Enrolments (SCE). EAs and SCEs are long-term agreements that provide additional benefits and

pricing advantages based on the volume of Azure services consumed.

It's important to note that Azure pricing can change over time, as Microsoft regularly updates and adjusts its pricing structure. To get accurate and up-to-date pricing information for Azure services, it's recommended to visit the official Microsoft Azure website or contact Microsoft sales representatives who can provide detailed pricing based on your specific requirements.

Azure Cloud Negotiation

Negotiating Microsoft Azure cloud costs can be a complex process, but here are some steps to take that will help your organisation navigate the negotiation process:

1. Understand your cloud requirements: Determine the type and volume of resources you need, anticipated usage patterns, and desired service levels. This will help you accurately assess your needs and negotiate the right pricing.

2. Assess your current usage: Review your existing cloud usage patterns and identify areas where you may be over-provisioned or underutilizing resources.

Optimizing your usage can help reduce costs and can provide leverageable insights during negotiations.

3. Optimize resource allocation: Review your resource allocation and make sure you are only using the necessary resources. This could involve rightsizing instances, automating resource allocation, or using scaling features to match your workload demands.

4. Prepare a business case: Develop a strong business case that outlines the reasons for negotiating lower cloud costs. This could include factors such as financial constraints, competitive pricing from other cloud providers, or the potential for increased usage over time in return for better pricing.

5. Engage in direct communication: Initiate direct discussions with your Microsoft sales representative or account manager. Clearly articulate your goals, concerns, and the specific cost reduction measures you are seeking. Be prepared to negotiate and provide supporting evidence for each of your requests.

6. Explore pricing models: Microsoft offers various pricing models for cloud services, such as consumption, service tiers, reserved instances, and volume discounts. Evaluate the pricing models available and determine which one best aligns with your usage patterns and cost-saving goals.

7. Consider long-term commitments: Microsoft may offer additional discounts or other incentives for customers who are willing to commit to longer-term contracts. Evaluate whether a multi-year agreement could provide cost savings or other benefits for your organization.

8. Bundle services: Microsoft often offers bundled solutions that include multiple cloud services or products. Explore the possibility of bundling services to potentially negotiate better pricing compared to purchasing services separately.

9. Leverage your relationship: If you have an existing relationship with Microsoft, emphasize the historic value you bring as a customer and the potential for future business. Highlight any positive experiences, references, or referrals that can strengthen your negotiating position.

10. Monitor competitive pricing: Stay updated on the market and competitive pricing for similar cloud services. If you come across better pricing from other cloud providers, leverage that information during negotiations to encourage Microsoft to offer more favourable terms.

11. Review the final agreement: Carefully review any proposed agreement or changes to your cloud contract before accepting. Ensure that all negotiated

terms and pricing are accurately reflected in the final agreement.

Negotiating cloud costs with Microsoft requires careful consideration of your requirements, diligent research, and effective communication.

Azure Discounting

The range of discounts an enterprise can get when buying Microsoft's Azure cloud services can vary depending on several factors, including the enterprise's consumption level, commitment term, payment option, and whether you are negotiating with Microsoft or one of their authorized resellers. Microsoft offers various pricing models and programs for Azure, and the specific discounts can be influenced by these factors.

Here are a few factors that can affect the discounts:

1. Consumption Level: Microsoft has introduced different pricing tiers based on the level of Azure usage. Higher consumption levels should qualify an enterprise for better volume discounts.

2. Commitment Term: Enterprises that commit to longer-term agreements, such as Azure Reserved Instances or Azure Hybrid Benefit, can often receive better discounts. These agreements require a commitment to using Azure services for a specific duration, typically one or three years.

3. Payment Option: Choosing the right payment option can also impact discounts. Microsoft offers different payment options, such as pay-as-you-go, monthly billing, or pre-paid plans. Pre-paying for services may provide additional discounts.

4. Negotiation: For larger enterprises or organizations with unique requirements, negotiations with Microsoft or authorized resellers can result in customized pricing and discounts. These negotiations can be influenced by factors such as the scale of the enterprise, strategic partnerships, or long-term commitments.

The specific discount ranges for Azure are not publicly disclosed by Microsoft, as they can vary based on the individual circumstances and negotiations. To determine the exact range of discounts available, it is recommended you contact Microsoft or an authorized reseller or an independent Consultant with experience of negotiating Microsoft Azure contracts directly, to discuss your organization's specific needs and usage patterns, and explore the negotiation options available.

Cloud Contract Nuances

Here are some other Microsoft Azure Cloud contract terms you should pay attention to in your Microsoft Cloud agreement as these can all affect the price you have to pay:

- **Avoid Paying Full Price Before Actual Usage:** The most common mistake companies make when signing Microsoft Azure Cloud agreements is starting to pay the full price before they start using all the services. For example, if you were to sign a three-year contract and started paying full price from day one, but only go fully live in the second year, you've essentially wasted up to 30% of your contract spend. This is the area where you can save a lot of money when negotiating a Microsoft Azure Cloud agreement, so take your time with it and keep it front and centre in your negotiation demands.

> ***Negotiation Tip:*** *To avoid this, it's crucial to clearly understand when you're going to go live. Always factor in a time buffer for potential delays. You can negotiate a rollout phase in your Microsoft Azure Cloud agreement, specifying how much your cloud contract will be spent in the first six months, the next six months, and the following years. You could also negotiate a services delay contract term, which means your contract and associated fees will not start until a later date.*

- Enable product mix rebalancing: During the Contract term, your requirements may well change, so try to include some form of no-cost product mix rebalancing in your Microsoft Azure Cloud agreement. This would allow you to shift some of your investment to different Microsoft Azure Cloud services to ensure the contract mirrors your changing needs.

- Renewal Price Cap: As standard a Microsoft Azure Cloud contract has no price caps in it. This means that when it comes to renewal time, the prices can leap up at Microsoft's discretion. So aim to get a renewal time price cap of perhaps no more than 3% baked into your Microsoft Azure Cloud contract.

Microsoft's Cloud Competitors:

Competition is always a great way to squeeze any vendor. Microsoft knows that its customers have a choice of Cloud suppliers, so a little competitive threat can often encourage Microsoft to move on price in order to retain the business.

But do bear in mind that if your organisation chooses an alternate Cloud provider to host your Microsoft software, such as Google, IBM or AWS, then you should check whether Microsoft has different licensing rules for running Microsoft software on other Cloud platforms, as such rules could affect the way you use its software and the price you pay for it. So do your homework and ensure you are aware of any cost or licensing implications of using another Cloud provider.

Other Cloud providers include:

1. Amazon Web Services (AWS) - A cloud computing platform that offers a wide range of services and features for businesses.

2. Google Cloud Platform - Provides a suite of cloud computing services including infrastructure, storage, and data analytics.

3. IBM Cloud - Offers a range of cloud computing solutions including infrastructure, storage, and AI services.

4. Oracle - Provides a range of cloud-based solutions including infrastructure, platform, and software services.

5. Alibaba Cloud - Provides a range of cloud services for businesses including infrastructure, storage, and data analytics.

Chapter 10

Negotiating Services Costs

<u>Steps to Take:</u>

Negotiating services and consulting costs with Microsoft can be a challenging task, but here are some steps that a business can take to navigate the negotiation process:

1. Define your project requirements: Clearly define the scope, timeline, and expected outcomes. This will help you accurately communicate your needs to Microsoft and negotiate the appropriate level of services.

2. Research alternative service providers: Compare their offerings, expertise, and pricing with Microsoft's services. Having alternative options can provide leverage during negotiations and help you negotiate better terms with Microsoft.

3. Evaluate your internal capabilities: Assess your organization's capabilities and determine if there are any tasks or expertise that can be handled internally. This can help reduce the scope and cost of services required from Microsoft.

4. Request a breakdown of costs: Ask Microsoft for a detailed breakdown of labour, travel expenses,

materials, and any other associated costs. This will enable you to understand how the costs are allocated and identify areas where you may have room for negotiation.

5. Leverage your relationship: If you have an existing Services relationship with Microsoft, leverage that to negotiate better terms. Highlight your total spend with Microsoft over the last 5 or 10 years, as well as any positive experiences, references, or successful projects that can strengthen your negotiating position.

6. Determine project milestones and payment terms: Consider structuring payments based on the completion of specific deliverables or phases, rather than paying upfront or in large lump sums. This can provide you with leverage and ensure that payments are tied to the progress of the project.

7. Negotiate resource allocation: Discuss resource allocation with Microsoft and identify opportunities to optimize costs. For example, you could explore options for using a hybrid mix of Microsoft, Microsoft Partners, as well as onshore and offshore resources to reduce costs.

8. Evaluate deliverables and warranties: Ensure that they align with your project requirements and that you are not being charged for unnecessary or

redundant deliverables. Negotiate any changes or modifications as needed.

9. Seek flexibility in pricing: Look at volume discounts, fixed-fee arrangements, or cost caps to mitigate project/cost overruns. Microsoft may be willing to accommodate such requests to secure your business.

10. Review the final agreement: Carefully review the final agreement or changes to your existing Services contract before accepting. Ensure that all negotiated terms, pricing, and deliverables are accurately reflected in the final paperwork.

Negotiating Services and Consulting costs with Microsoft requires thorough planning, effective communication, and a clear understanding of your project requirements. Be prepared to negotiate, explore alternative options, and advocate for your organization's needs throughout the negotiation process.

Services Discounts

The range of discounts an enterprise can get when buying Microsoft's consulting or professional services can vary depending on the scope and duration of the project, the level of engagement required, the volume of services being purchased, historic discounts, and any existing agreements or negotiations with Microsoft.

Microsoft offers a range of consulting and professional services, including implementation, migration, customization, training, and support services. The pricing for these services can be customized based on the specific requirements of the enterprise.

While the specific discount ranges for Microsoft's consulting and professional services are not publicly disclosed, enterprises may have the opportunity to negotiate pricing based on factors such as:

1. Project Scope and Duration: The complexity and duration of the project can influence the negotiation of pricing and potential discounts. Large-scale and long-term projects may have more room for negotiation.

2. Volume of Services: Enterprises that require a significant volume of consulting or professional services may be eligible for volume-based discounts. This could be relevant for enterprises with multiple projects or ongoing engagements with Microsoft.

3. Existing Agreements or Partnerships: If the enterprise has an existing agreement or partnership with Microsoft, such as an Enterprise Agreement (EA) or a strategic partnership, they may be able to leverage those relationships to negotiate better pricing or discounts for consulting or professional services.

4. Customized Engagement: Enterprises with unique or specific requirements may have the opportunity to negotiate pricing based on the tailored nature of the engagement. This could include customization, specialized training, or dedicated support.

It is recommended to reach out to Microsoft directly or connect with authorized Microsoft partners to discuss the specific requirements of the enterprise and explore the negotiation options available for pricing and discounts on consulting or professional services.

Chapter 11

Bringing It All Together

Negotiate the Total Price.

Once you have squeezed each element of the deal (Software, Support, Cloud, Services), then squeeze the Total Price of all of the cumulative parts.

For example, let's say you have negotiated each element separately and have arrived at a total net price of £3.6m. This last step is to then challenge Microsoft on the £3.6m number and demand they reduce it to something lower, e.g., £3.4m.

> ***Negotiation Tip:*** *If you haven't already escalated your negotiation above your Microsoft Sales Rep, then this is the time to do that. Going to the Sales Manager, Country Manager, Regional Vice President or even Microsoft's Head Office can often pay dividends for large deal negotiations. The focus at this late stage is all about getting some extra final reduction in the Total Price. Often an Executive-level conversation is required to make this happen between your CIO and a senior Microsoft Executive.*

Negotiating Beyond Price.

Once Microsoft has stopped conceding on price, then a savvy buyer will look to obtain further non-financial concessions.

These concessions can vary depending on the specific circumstances, the scope of the agreement, and the relationship between Microsoft and the customer.

Here are some examples of other concessions Microsoft may consider:

1.   Extended payment terms: Microsoft may offer extended payment terms, allowing the customer to spread out payments over a longer period. This can help alleviate immediate financial burdens and provide more flexibility in managing cash flow.

2.   Additional free Training and Support: Microsoft could provide additional free Training or Support resources to help customers maximize the value of their Microsoft products or services. This can include access to training materials, workshops, or dedicated Support personnel.

3.   Customization or tailored solutions: In certain cases, Microsoft may be willing to customize their products or services to better align with the customer's specific requirements. This can involve

modifications, integrations, or enhancements to better suit the customer's unique needs.

4. Proof-of-concept (POC) or trial periods: Microsoft might offer a POC or free trial period for certain products or services. This allows customers to test the solution before committing fully, reducing the risk and providing an opportunity to evaluate its effectiveness in their specific environment.

5. Access to beta programs or early releases: Microsoft may grant customers access to beta programs or early releases of their products, enabling them to gain early insights and potentially influence product development.

6. Partnership or co-marketing opportunities: In some cases, Microsoft may want to explore partnership or co-marketing opportunities with the customer. This can involve joint promotional activities, participation in marketing campaigns, or showcasing the customer's success story. If Microsoft wants this, and the customer is willing to entertain it, then Microsoft should offer some form of value or concession to the customer in return.

7. ECIF: Another way Microsoft can sweeten an Enterprise deal is to offer their customers some additional funding/credit to help pay for Microsoft related services. As part of the negotiation process, customers should ask Microsoft to allocate some

money via their 'End Customer Investment Funds' (ECIF) program (formerly known as Business Investment Funds (BIF) or Customer Investment Funds (CIF)). This program allows Microsoft to set-aside funding (often in the form of a credit note) which customers can draw on to pay for services from Microsoft or a Microsoft Partner. For example, a couple of ways such funds could be used might be to help transition from Office on-premise to Office 365, or from one competitive CRM vendor to Microsoft's Dynamics 365 CRM suite. So long as the money/credit is spent supporting the Microsoft estate, then that's how you can use an ECIF.

It's important to note that the concessions Microsoft is willing to provide can vary, and their availability depends on factors such as the size and strategic importance of the customer, the competitive landscape, and the specific negotiation dynamics and timing of the deal.

Chapter 12

Post Sale

Post-Negotiation Relationships are Important.

Effective post-negotiation relationship management can help to build trust and create a foundation for future collaborations and negotiations.

It is important to continue to communicate openly with Microsoft, even after the negotiation is complete. This can include providing updates on the progress of the agreement, sharing feedback and addressing any concerns that may arise.

Additionally, it is important to maintain a respectful and professional demeanour, even if disagreements arise or there are unexpected issues with the agreement. This can help to prevent misunderstandings and ensure that the relationship remains positive over the long term.

Strategies for Maintaining Good Relationships with Microsoft

Here are some strategies for maintaining good relationships with Microsoft after the negotiation:

1. Follow through on commitments: If you made any promises or commitments during the negotiation, be sure to follow through on them in a timely and effective manner.

2. Stay in touch: Send occasional updates on relevant Company developments or news, or perhaps invite them to your industry events.

3. Look for future opportunities: Be on the lookout for future opportunities to work together or collaborate. Keep the lines of communication open and be open to exploring new opportunities.

4. Resolve disputes professionally: If any disputes arise after the negotiation, handle them professionally and with respect. Work to find mutually agreeable solutions that benefit both parties.

By following these strategies, you can maintain good relationships with Microsoft after the negotiation and set the foundation for future collaboration and success.

Dealing with Potential Conflicts

Even with the best intentions and efforts, conflicts can still arise post-negotiation.

Here are some strategies for dealing with potential conflicts:

1. Acknowledge the conflict: Ignoring a conflict won't make it go away. It's essential to acknowledge the conflict and identify the underlying issues causing it.

2. Stay calm: Keep your emotions in check and avoid escalating the situation.

3. Listen actively: Listen to Microsoft's perspective, and then try to understand their point of view. Avoid interrupting them or dismissing their concerns.

4. Identify common ground: Look for areas where both parties can agree, and then try to find a mutually acceptable solution.

5. Seek third-party assistance: If the conflict cannot be resolved between the parties, consider seeking the assistance of a mediator or arbitrator.

Dealing with conflicts after a negotiation can be challenging, but it's crucial to address them promptly and effectively to maintain a positive business relationship.

Chapter 13

Negotiating Audits

<u>Audits Are Inevitable</u>

As stated in Microsoft's contracts, they have a right to audit a customer's use of their products. This is a reasonable request as Microsoft has spent a lot of money developing products and the embedded Intellectual Property (IP), and they want to protect that IP as well as ensure customers pay for all the products they are using.

If Microsoft suspects that a customer may be non-compliant and might be using products they haven't paid for, then Microsoft's will initiate the audit by sending the customer a letter stating their intent to conduct a license audit.

If their audit then finds non-compliance, then the customer will be asked to pay for any discrepancies in licensing and may also be asked to pay an additional financial penalty if the non-compliance is large or has been on-going for some time.

The Importance of SAM

It's essential for all Microsoft customers to accurately monitor and track their Microsoft software usage to ensure compliance and to avoid audit issues.

There are many Software Asset Management (SAM) tools available from independent SAM specialists that can help with this process. Ideally the SAM tool is designed specifically for Microsoft and keeps up to date with all the latest Microsoft licensing nuances.

As well as helping stay compliant, SAM can also provide usage data and associated information that in some circumstance can help a customer rebuff a Microsoft audit claim, or at least provide some leverage to push back on Microsoft's non-compliance claims.

Negotiating An Audit:

Negotiating an audit outcome with Microsoft can be a challenging process. Here are key steps to take when engaging in an audit outcome negotiation:

1. Understand the audit findings: Thoroughly review the audit findings, including any non-compliance issues or discrepancies identified by

Microsoft. Gain a clear understanding of the specific areas of concern and the basis for their claims.

2. **Conduct an internal review:** Conduct an internal review of your licensing and usage practices to validate or refute Microsoft's findings. Compare Microsoft's non-compliance claims to the output of your own SAM tools. Verify the accuracy of Microsoft's claims, assess any potential licensing gaps, and identify any mitigating factors that may impact the audit outcome.

3. **Determine financial exposure:** Assess the financial implications of the audit findings, including any potential licensing shortfalls, penalties, or backdated fees.

4. **Engage with Microsoft promptly:** Initiate communication with Microsoft as soon as possible to address the audit findings. Promptly responding to Microsoft's audit results demonstrates your willingness to engage in the process and can help set the stage for more favourable negotiations.

5. **Seek contractual clarifications:** Review the terms of your existing licensing agreement and seek clarification on any ambiguous or unclear terms that may have contributed to the audit findings. Use the negotiation to establish clearer guidelines and ensure future compliance.

6. Seek professional advice: Consider engaging legal counsel or independent licensing experts experienced in Microsoft audits. They can provide valuable insights, guidance, and help protect your organization's interests during the negotiation process.

7. Prepare a detailed response: Develop a comprehensive response that addresses each audit finding individually. Provide evidence, documentation, and explanations to support your position and challenge any inaccuracies or misunderstandings.

8. Identify potential mitigating factors: Highlight any mitigating factors that may impact the audit outcome, such as licensing agreements, contractual terms, or usage patterns that may have changed since the audited period. Emphasize any efforts taken to rectify non-compliance, if applicable.

9. Explore options for resolution: Discuss possible resolutions with Microsoft, including options for remediation, voluntary compliance, or alternative licensing arrangements.

10. Negotiate terms and penalties: Engage in negotiation discussions with Microsoft to reach mutually acceptable terms and penalties. Consider exploring options for reducing penalties, extending payment terms, or structuring a settlement that aligns with your organization's financial capabilities.

11. Document the final agreement: Once the audit negotiations are concluded, document the agreed-upon terms, penalties, and any adjustments made to the licensing agreement. Ensure that both parties have a clear understanding of the outcomes and any ongoing obligations.

Microsoft audit negotiations can be intricate, and it's important to approach the process with careful preparation, transparency, and a willingness to find a mutually beneficial resolution.

> **Negotiation tip:** While Microsoft has the right to audit a customer's use of their products at any time, some buyers have got Microsoft to agree an amendment to their EA contract to not audit within the first year of the EA. This is a sensible move if your organisation has a lot going on in the first twelve months of the EA and don't want to be distracted by a Microsoft audit in that time.

Chapter 14

Conclusion

Negotiating with Microsoft can be a daunting task, but with the right preparation and planning, you can secure a deal that benefits your organization.

Don't wait until the last minute! Begin your preparations at least six months prior to your Microsoft contract renewal date to ensure you have ample time to explore all possibilities.

Ideally you should start your negotiation preparation twelve months out from the date you plan to conclude the negotiation. Leaving negotiations to the eleventh hour puts all the bargaining power in Microsoft's hands, likely resulting in higher costs and potential overspending on unnecessary products.

Rest assured; your Microsoft sales representative will have been meticulously preparing for your contract negotiation well in advance. They will have been closely monitoring your license usage and actively encouraging your users to explore new Microsoft products and services. They will be determined to expand your existing Microsoft footprint and drive revenue growth.

To level the playing field, it's essential for you to match their efforts and conduct thorough research, planning and preparation.

Collaborate with your IT and Technical teams to gain a deep understanding of your organization's current use of and need for Microsoft products and services. Use your SAM tools to help identify actual usage and to perhaps harvest unused licenses. Projecting your future needs over the next three years is equally important.

Gather market intelligence from all sources to help shape your thinking and planning. Talk to your Microsoft Partner, market Analysts and Research firms, and your peers via Microsoft user groups. Find out what they are doing and what they recommend.

Consider engaging with an independent Microsoft negotiation expert to help guide you through the process.

IT budgets are often tight, so it's vital to optimize your spending with Microsoft by acquiring only what your organization truly needs, precisely when it needs it, and only at the best possible price.

© Mark Bartrick 2023

Milton Keynes UK
Ingram Content Group UK Ltd.
UKHW020644260923
429409UK00015B/856